Green and
Profitable

BOOK 4

The New Realities of 21st Century Business

Shel Horowitz

Green and Profitable Book 4: The New Realities of 21st Century Businesss
©2015, Shel Horowitz

ISBN-13: 978-1511419550
ISBN-10: 1511419555

Printed in the United States of America
10, 9, 8, 7, 6, 5, 4, 3, 2

Published by AWM Books - Hadley, MA

Contents

Can One Community Self–Sufficiency Initiative Really Do All This?

What if a single action could: get troubled teens off the streets and into something productive—and develop their entrepreneurship skills in the process...provide fresh local organic food to inner-city people with no other access to quality produce...clean up a blighted neighborhood vacant lot and spark a caring community spirit? What if that action could be done without any significant government or corporate resources, other than a space to have it?

Sound like a lot to do at once? Oddly enough, it's probably easier to create a single action that accomplishes multiple goods than to create a program that requires massive intravenous injections of outside aid to address only one of those goals. (And this is a sustainability principle that's true in many areas: energy, transportation, manufacturing, and more.)

This particular set of objectives can all be met by creating urban community gardens, and any business owner can benefit by facilitating their creation. Your own property values go up, risk of crime and vandalism goes down, and you add to your standing in your home community.

All you need to do is find some neighborhood leaders who'll get the project going, and provide a quarter-acre or so of unused land (ideally, a parcel that can be expanded as the project succeeds)—or even an appropriately engineered rooftop.

Successes are happening all over the country.[1] A few among many:

25 kids, ages 9-17, run the Brightmoor Youth Garden on Detroit's west side, start to finish. Last year, they planted, maintained, harvested and sold 1,300 pounds—$2,700 worth of—produce. And this is only one of numerous local food projects in Detroit.[2]

In Richmond, California (near San Francisco), a community group called Urban Tilth has two farms based at schools and is planning to hire 26 kids to plant and manage an orchard. One of these farms involves 30 students in a class called "Urban Ecology and Food Systems," whose curriculum integrates lessons from the garden into the classroom.[3]

The city of Cleveland, hit hard by the recession, has 3,300 acres of vacant land and 15,000 vacant buildings within city limits. Rather than blast big swaths through the neighborhoods in the traditional urban renewal "solutions," the city is reclaiming 15 parcels in a pilot project to grow its own food—adding to the 175 community gardens and 40 for-profit market gardens already in existence. Bobbi Reichtell, senior vice president for programs of Neighborhood Progress Inc. (the group coordinating the effort) has an ambitious goal: returning $800 million a year to the local economy by raising the percentage of locally grown food in Cleveland from 2 percent to 10 percent.[4]

Nuestras Raices, a longstanding community group in depressed Holyoke, Massachusetts, has started an urban farm and several spin-off businesses. As its farmers gain skills in the business world, the organization helps them start mini-farms of their own, and new farmers take their place on the original land.[5] Interestingly enough, Nuestras Raices itself was founded by a group of community gardeners.

In Portland, Oregon, 3000 residents work the city's community gardens, and another 1000 are on a waiting list.[6]

On the rooftops of the neighborhood once written off as "Fort Apache," Sustainable South Bronx is growing food, extending the lives of the buildings, and slashing energy use.[7]

If this multiplicity of benefits could make a huge difference in your community, consider helping one get started. Maybe your corporate headquarters has a sunny section of lawn that could become garden space (and perhaps reduce the health risks to your employees from pesticide use)—or your retail location has an unused roof. Do you happen to have a skilled gardener on staff who'd like to volunteer a few hours to train neighborhood kids and get the project going? Can such an initiative tie in to zero-waste, buy-local or other green projects you're already doing?

And can *you* benefit by branding your firm in your community as an advocate for jobs, entrepreneurship, improving the environment, healthy fresh food, and re-skilling our youth?

Asking for Help from the Cloud Crowd

Compare the before- and after-versions of this three-minute video promoting my "Making Green Sexy" speech:

BEFORE: youtu.be/FtghtR8lcrY

AFTER: youtu.be/DByWN4Feaj0

How did I know how to improve it? I asked on the cloud.

For nearly 20 years, when I want feedback on an idea or a project, help choosing book covers or titles, or recommendations on service providers, one of the places I turn to is the cloud. It's certainly not the only place I go for feedback and advice—but consistently, I get very useful help.

I started participating in online discussion groups in 1994, back when the only groups I'd experienced online were discussion boards on AOL. By 1995, I was exploring online groups on the wider Internet.

Over the years, I've joined dozens. Often, I unsubscribe again within a few months or a couple of years. But there are groups I participate in that I've been involved with since the 20th century. Some of these are organized by industry (green marketing, book publishing, speaking, etc.), some are general business discussion lists. Some are moderated (where an administrator has to approve each post); some are open.

Advice quality will vary. Often, there will be a mixture of great and terrible, and it's up to you to sort the difference.

And that's one of the reasons why it helps to participate actively on a list for a while before asking for this kind of help. First, this makes you a known quantity, someone who has helped others and therefore incites others to reciprocate when you need help; you'll get more, and better, responses. And second, it gives you the judgment to recognize who knows what they're talking about and who's just winging it.

It was a publishing group, years ago, that convinced me not to go to press with the title "Win-Win Marketing." I had asked for help choosing between two subtitles, and was told by several people I respect that my main title had implications I  didn't want. It took two months to come up with the right title for that book, which finally went to press as "Principled Profit: Marketing That Puts People First"—a much better title. (Ironically enough, the book's Spanish-language publisher in Mexico—without ever knowing about its almost-title—dubbed it "Mercadotechnia Basada en Ganar-Ganar," which literally translates as "Marketing Based in Win-Win." Maybe the same negative baggage doesn't apply in Mexican culture.)

For feedback on the speaker video, I posted to several discussion lists on green business, general marketing, and local business in my area. I got far and away the most useful (and the largest number of) comments from a LinkedIn discussion group called "Step Into the

Spotlight," where I happen to be quite active. I received several public and a few private responses that were quite helpful.

Responses broke down in to three categories:

- ✓ Suggested improvements that were useful and easy to implement

- ✓ Suggested improvements that would improve the video but would be too hard to implement because I didn't have the right footage available

- ✓ Suggestions I did not feel would improve the video

Among the advice I accepted: move the 33% ROI bit higher, get rid of some of the slow parts, insert some audience shots (my video producer found only one usable one in all my footage), rerecord the voiceovers around the two endorsements and cut down the verbiage on those slides, drop some of my narrative in places, and fix an audio quality issue in one section that I hadn't even noticed.

Suggestions I'd have liked to do couldn't easily enough: reducing the number of times I blink (my eyes are very sensitive to environmental irritants, and I blink a lot)—and fixing a word order issue that would have required replacing actual audio from one of my speeches with a new recording.

One of the suggestions I rejected entirely was that audiences can't handle the idea of three different types of audiences for green products and services. I disagree; in fact, I would not feel I delivered value if I spent a whole 60- or 90-minute speech making just one or two points. I don't want people in the audience to feel like they've been hit by a water cannon, but at the same time, I want them to come away feeling they know more, understand more, and have multiple tools in their own tool boxes that they can implement in their own marketing.

Once again, this sort of informal focus group proved its worth to me. In my mind, the later version is a vast improvement.

Next month: how to use these types of discussion lists to grow your business.

Look Outside Your Box: What Can Other Industries and Other Environments Teach You About Synergy

Would you believe a powerful green business was inspired by the space program? Believe it.

Swedish entrepreneur Mehrdad Mahdjoubi thought about how little water astronauts use in space and how much of their water gets recycled; he wondered why we couldn't adapt that water use pattern to our own households.

The result? The OrbSys: A shower that uses only 3 percent of the water and 20 percent of the energy of a typical shower, while claiming to produce higher comfort and better sanitation (note the appeal on multiple benefits). Mahdjoubi claims typical users could save $1000 per year.

By recycling most of the water, much less is needed. But the extra benefit was that much less energy is required as well, *because the water going back into the showerhead is already hot from its first pass.* If you've ever stood to the side as a whole lot of cold water came out of the showerhead before it was warm enough to step under, you know exactly why this is important. (Read more about

Mahdjoubi and the OrbSys at http://ow.ly/ruUW2 and many other places; he's good at getting publicity.)

Remember this, too: the first or even the second categories of drive-through businesses weren't restaurants; they were banks, starting in 1930, and car washes, beginning later that decade. Some smart person looked outside the box and thought, "if people appreciate being able to bank from their cars, maybe they'd like to get their food handed to them in their cars, too." And by 1948, there was at least one drive-through eatery. Since then, the model has spread to other industries as well, including dry-cleaners and at least one wedding chapel.

While drive-through businesses aren't particularly eco-friendly, it's easy to find other examples within the green world.

Think about the spiral of creativity that started with shopping carts. Inventor Sylvan Goldman was inspired to create the first in-store shopping cart (patented in 1937) by looking at a folding chair (itself a wonderful space-saving, and thus green, invention). Someone else studied his invention and figured out

that a version shoppers could take home would be very helpful for urban dwellers who might not be able to park right next to their house (or might not own a car).

Someone else thought about substituting bicycles for delivery trucks, perhaps after watching a shopper pull a cart through a crowded street while cars and trucks were stuck in traffic. Someone else discovered bicycles could be adapted for other industrial uses, even trash hauling.

All of these innovations reduce the number of car and truck trips. And that makes them green.

Another great green example is the whole phenomenon of upcycling: turning waste materials into consumer products. Think about the leap of consciousness to see a bunch of old computer chips, vinyl records, or bicycle parts (to name three popular raw materials used in upcycling)  and imagine them as works of art, or home decor, or home furnishings, or jewelry, or clothing. My daughter's purse and my wallet used to be automobile tires. We own a couple of tote bags that had past lives as plastic soda bottles. Recycled, repurposed material shows up in kitchen counters, decking and fencing, building materials, clothing, garden aids, and all sorts of other places.

In short, as a culture, we have begun to learn to ask the key question: "now that I'm done with the original purpose, what else can this be used for?"

Of course, this is not a new conversation—there's a decades-old expression: "Use it up, wear it out, make it do or do without," and a long and honorable tradition of repurposing extending to every area of life, even musical instruments made of old oil drums. But what's different is that upcycling has become mainstream. Repurposing is no longer just for frugality geeks or environmental activists; it has even penetrated the elegant boutiques that cater to fashion-conscious upscale consumers. Yes, green is now chic. Recycled and upcycled products are "in" now.

And you as a green business owner should be paying careful attention to this trend, and how it can benefit your business.

A Pessimist and an Optimist

Just as I was pondering what to write about in this month's column, I went to a pair of lectures organized by Nerd Nite Northampton (yep—that's how they spell it).

The juxtaposition of the two talks was striking. I don't know if the organizers considered this aspect—but one was very optimistic, and the other quite pessimistic about living here on Planet Earth.

The optimist, photojournalist Greg Saulmon, took us on a tour of the amazing birds of urban, industrial Holyoke and Springfield, Massachusetts: snowy owls, spotted owls, Cooper's and redtail hawks, bald eagles, peregrine falcons, and a host of smaller birds. His stunning photography captured a pair of raptors on the roof of an

industrial building, framed by a plume of steam. He caught birds doing acrobatics and birds speeding through the air. Birds on building gutters and an owl in the back yard of a woman who thanked him for being in the news media and wanting to report something other than a shooting.

His message was simple: nature is all around us, even in cities—and our kids can learn to love it. We can create effective habitat for both wild animals and people, even in the toughest inner-city neighborhoods.

As a New York City native, I concur. Watching Saulmon's talk, "The Birds Downtown," I kept thinking about my own childhood in a far more urban place than Holyoke, and how much nature I experienced even in one of the largest cities in the country.

Many of my earliest encounters with nature were within the city limits—in the parks and on the beaches, of course—but also in the plane trees that lined many city streets (dwarfed though they were by the giant buildings around them), and the little oases of parkland. Noticing the different grasses growing along an abandoned railroad track, tromping through city parks with my high school biology teacher as he led a tree identification walk, observing squirrels, and even going hawk-watching with my mom at the Pelham Bay Landfill, just a mile from our 20th floor apartment in a 26-storey high-rise, part of a complex of 33 high-rise apartment buildings tucked into a corner of the Bronx.

This neighborhood of 58,000 people was not important enough to get a subway extension, or even to make a new station on the commuter rail line that bordered the project. But while it may not have gotten on the radar of city planners, it definitely did get on the radar of the migrating birds. The buildings were spaced some distance apart from each other, and there was a lot of open land. Active marshlands bordered the community, and the Hutchinson River and Long Island Sound lay just beyond. A resident colony of geese acted like they owned the place, and gulls were always swooping around.

So if you live in a city—help your kids, or the kids who live near you appreciate nature. The first step in saving the world is awareness, and you can be part of that.

The second talk of the evening was much less upbeat. Filmmaker Ian Cheney's "The End of Darkness" focused on a part of nature that's slipping away rapidly: a night sky dark enough to see thousands of stars.

Growing up in New York City, there was so much light pollution that I never knew what the sky is supposed to look like. Cheney described a New York City native who thought the Hayden Planetarium sky show was a hoax. And I can understand that,  because when I used to walk home from the subway at night—a mile walk along an eight-lane highway—I'd never seen more stars than I could count—usually few enough that I could actually count them on my fingers. And living in a rural area for many years now, I'm still amazed when I look up on a clear night and see thousands of little dots of light.

But star deprivation, says Cheney, isn't just an aesthetic issue; it has severe consequences for our own and other species. Two among several examples: 1. Sea turtle hatchlings have evolved to head toward the brightest thing they see when they emerge at night from their eggs—because, historically, the ocean, catching the moonlight in its water, was brighter than the land. But now, if their mothers bury the eggs near a coastal city like Miami, the turtle babies head downtown, and die before they find the ocean.

The human example is even more disturbing; there seems to be a correlation between the false daylight of our populated areas—and breast cancer. Cheney doesn't have a solution—but he knows we need to look at this as a society.

Failure is *Always* an Option

I laugh whenever I hear that famous phrase, "failure is not an option." It shows not only enormous ignorance of the real world and the human brain, but also enormous hubris.

Let's get real. Failure is always an option—with sufficient bad luck or timing, loss of motivation, key player defections, or inadequate funding. This doesn't mean the task is impossible; it's just that currently, for whatever reason, it doesn't seem worth marshaling the necessary resources to finish the task.

Sometimes, we can minimize the impact of choosing failure. Almost always, we can embrace it as a learning opportunity.

The trick is to fail cheaply and early—and maybe often, make your mistakes, and move on. See what can be salvaged, what can be reinvented, and what should be thrown in the trash. Thomas Edison took 10,000 steps to invent the light bulb. Most people would say he failed 9999 times. He saw it not as a failure but as a 10,000-step process. In other words, our failures teach us enough to achieve our successes.

I've had my share of failures. This spring, for example, I set up a telesummit involving 17 speakers, plus eight bonus calls from my archives for those who purchased the recording package. I spent some money and a considerable amount of time.

And it failed.

The business model is proven. I just got a mailing from the organizer of another telesummit, and she reported 2500 signups and a 5% conversion to the paid recording package. If I'd had those numbers, I would have made a profit even after paying 50% commissions to the speakers who brought in those buyers. But I was not able to motivate people to visit, sign up, and buy.

What did she do differently? First, she had a much broader-based subject appeal. There are a lot more people who want to succeed as book authors than in running a green business. Second, she had more speakers. And third, she motivated all her participants with leaderboards and contests and a general sense that things were really moving and we all would want to get on the bandwagon.

While I was expecting a revenue stream instead of a cost center, I learned enormously from this failure. Among other things, I learned not to count on your speakers promoting your event in a meaningful way. Some of the largest list owners never mailed, and thus my traffic was far lower than expected. Low enough that the sales were basically invisible.

Here are some of my other takeaways:

1) Learn when to work with off-the-shelf products and when to go custom. I could have done 90 percent of what I wanted to with an off-the-shelf software package called Instant Teleseminar. But their model involves paying every month, forever— so instead, I just hired someone to build the

functionality I was looking for. That decision led to some serious cost overruns, and I still didn't achieve all the functionality I wanted. If the summit had succeeded and I did a new one every six or 12 months, developing the in-house solution still would have been the right decision, because it would probably pay for itself around the fourth summit. But since I doubt I'll organize another series like this one—though I might very well reuse the content I created and rerun the series at some point—I should have just bought the product.

2) Keep it simple! The website is beautiful, but it's too hard to use. I think it scared people off. I should have really improved the usability before I let it go live.

3) Identify an audience of buyers. The woman who achieved that big telesummit success could draw from tens of millions of people who want to be successful published authors. While there are hundreds of thousands who want to run successful green businesses, maybe that isn't a critical mass, especially since I didn't have a direct channel to reach them.

4) Keep the content focused. I think my series split its energy between being about marketing, generally, and being about green business success. This may not have been wise. Maybe I needed to push more of the marketing experts to speak specifically about applying their techniques in the green world.

5)

Impossible is a Dare: Business For a Better World

Well into the 21st century, isn't it time to finally say goodbye to the big crises that hold our whole society back? We should no longer have to put up with hunger, poverty, war, violence, and catastrophic climate change.

And here comes the outcry: "we've always suffered with these things. It's impossible to make them go away."

Well, guess what: we actually already know how to eliminate or greatly reduce most of the biggest problems the world faces.

And consider this: we do hundreds of things every day that were considered "impossible" not all that long ago.

When my house was built, in 1743, we assumed that humans couldn't travel faster than the fastest horse. Yet the International Space Station hurtles astronauts through space at 17,247 miles per hour. When I was born, in 1956, most people—if they had a phone at all—shared one phone, tethered by a wire to a wall, for a whole household, or sometimes several households. Most people had never even seen a computer, let alone owned one. Music came into our houses on big vinyl platters or over a staticky, low-fidelity radio. Apartheid reigned over South Africa, Rhodesia, and the American South, while communist dictatorships ruled Eastern Europe. And life expectancy was decades less than it is today.

Those are just a very few of the thousands of shifts we've made about what is possible, in less than 60 years.

In short, "impossible" is a mindset, a self-imposed limitation—and we can change it.

We've known this for years. Henry Ford said, "Whether you think you can do a thing or think you can't do a thing, you're right." Muhammad Ali put it this way: "Impossible is just a big word thrown around by small men who find it easier to live in the world they've been given than to explore the power they have to change it. Impossible is not a fact. It's an opinion. Impossible is not a declaration. It's a dare. Impossible is potential. Impossible is temporary. Impossible is nothing."

This quote struck me so deeply that I built my entire TEDx talk around it: www.business-for-a-better-world.com/tedtalks—and I'll bet if you spend 15 minutes listening to it, you'll be inspired.

A Personal Example

I have first-hand experience. Among several "impossible" achievements, I founded the mass movement that stopped a developer's plan to kill our local mountain by building a large housing project. While the "experts" were wringing their hands, we went out and got it done.

Here's a key insight: when you look deeply, a lot of the causes of hunger, poverty, war, violence, and catastrophic climate change turn out to be about resources: who uses how much, whether they're taken sustainably, how fairly they're distributed. When we address resources systemically, we're able to transform hunger and poverty into sufficiency, war and violence into peace, and catastrophic climate change into planetary balance—and helping individuals reclaim their power to actively create this better world.

And we actually know how to do this. We knew how to build near-zero net-energy buildings at least as far back as 1983. We understand how to significantly increase crop yields without using chemicals and without compromising quality. We've developed all sorts of conflict resolution techniques that don't involve shooting each other. And we know how to replace nearly all our fossil and nuclear fuels with the combination of clean, renewable energy and deep conservation, thus reversing the increase in greenhouse gases. We even know how to imitate nature's best engineers to achieve zero waste while developing stronger, lighter materials and incredible processes to o things like extract water out of fog, the way a certain beetle does.

Where we've gotten stuck, in other words, in not in the technology. It's in finding the political will to implement all this great stuff.

But now for the good news: we don't have to wait around for governments to get it done. *We can motivate the private sector, the business community, by showing them how to make a profit.* We've tried for too long to motivate social change through guilt and shame. Let's try the profit motive instead.

I intend to spend the next 10 to 15 years of my life creating this incredibly exciting world where humans can reach our potential without fear. Will you join me in this incredible journey?

Learn more at www.business-for-a-better-world.com

* * *

I enjoyed writing this column from 2010 to 2014, and I think I provided very high value for those who read it. Unfortunately, I never got enough markets to make the project economically viable.

As I move in the direction of helping companies see the value in solving problems like hunger, poverty, war, and climate catastrophe, I can no longer afford the luxury of doing this column for the few markets that subscribed. So this will be the last issue for a while.

I'd love to bring it back, if I can get to a minimum number of subscribers each paying just $10 per month. If you have possible markets for me, please drop me a line at shel AT greenandprofitable.com with the subject "Column Market."

Disclaimer: The very observant among you may notice that some examples come up more than once. Keep in mind that this ebook is a compilation of a monthly column that ran for four years. I have organized the columns by topic rather than chronologically here, and as a result, columns that may have been years apart end up close to each other in the same ebook. Yes, some examples are repeated, but they were inserted to make different points, at different times. Please also note that nothing in this ebook series should be taken as legal or professional advice, and as in any situation, your results may vary as you implement the tips and ideas.

About Shel Horowitz and Business For a Better World

Green business profitability expert Shel Horowitz shows businesses how to profit both by going green and by addressing problems like hunger and poverty, war, violence, and catastrophic climate change. Active in both marketing and the environment since his teen years in the early 1970s, Shel is the award-winning author of eight books including long-running Amazon category bestseller _Guerrilla Marketing Goes Green_.

- ✓ As a consultant, Shel brings laser focus to turning problems into opportunities, opening new markets, and helping you identify potential partners.

- ✓ As a marketing and informational copywriter trained in journalism, Shel is known for his clear writing, ability to make technical concepts accessible, and his skill in telling "the story behind the story" to move people to action.

- ✓ As an international speaker and trainer, Shel combines dynamic vocal style with powerful graphics and gets his audiences actively involved. He's spoken at major business and environmental conferences in locations as diverse as Istanbul, Davos (Switzerland), and Honolulu.

After over a decade actively assisting green businesses with their marketing, Shel branched out in 2014 to help businesses seize profit opportunities in turning hunger and poverty into sufficiency, war and violence into peace, and catastrophic climate change into planetary balance—and helping individuals reclaim their power to actively create this better world.

Shel is happy to talk to you about helping in any of these areas. Reach him at 413-586-2388 (8 a.m. to 10 p.m. US Eastern Time), email shel AT greenandprofitable.com, or find him on Twitter @ShelHorowitz.

Shel also has a gift for you: a free copy of his ebook, *Painless Green: 111 Tips to Help the Environment, Lower Your Carbon Footprint, Cut Your Budget, and Improve Your Quality of Life—With No Negative Impact on Your Lifestyle*. To claim your free copy of this $9.95 ebook, visit PainlessGreenBook.com/earthday and use the code, G&Pebook.

One more set of gifts, FREE with your no-cost subscription to Shel Horowitz's monthly Clean and Green Newsletter:

- ✓ Seven Tips to Gain Marketing Traction as a Green Guerrilla

- ✓ Seven Weeks to a Greener Business: once a week for seven weeks, tips on going greener with printing, energy saving, waste reduction, water conservation, transportation, going deep–green, and of course, green marketing.

- ✓ Plus the informative monthly newsletter, published since 1997 and featuring a business tip or profile plus a book review each issue.

Sign up in the upper-right-hand corner at http://greenandprofitable.com.

www.ingramcontent.com/pod-product-compliance
Lightning Source LLC
Chambersburg PA
CBHW070757180526
45168CB00004B/1649